$095

SIMPLE GUIDE TO

RUSSIA

CUSTOMS & ETIQUETTE

COVER ILLUSTRATION
Russian Icons

ABOUT THE AUTHOR

IRENE SLATTER teaches Russian at the University of
Durham, England, and is the author of the sister volume,
Very Simple Russian. She has been a frequent visitor to
Russia over the last 30 years with a wide circle of both
professional and personal acquaintances, and has a
special interest in the role of women in Russian society.

AUTHOR'S NOTE

Obtaining clear and correct information about Russia these days is
no longer easy. The situation can change from day to day and a
law or decree can be introduced or revoked which immediately
changes everything. This is as true in the area of economic reform
as it is in any area, which makes life confusing for Russians as well
as for foreign visitors. However, the information in this book is as
correct as I can get it up to the time of going to press.

I would like to thank my husband, Dr John Slatter, for his help
and encouragement in the preparation of this book.

ILLUSTRATED BY
IRENE SANDERSON

SIMPLE GUIDE TO

RUSSIA

CUSTOMS & ETIQUETTE

IRENE SLATTER

GLOBAL BOOKS LTD

Simple Guides • Series 1
CUSTOMS & ETIQUETTE

The Simple Guide to
RUSSIA
CUSTOMS & ETIQUETTE
by Irene Slatter

First edition published 1990
by Simple Books Ltd

Second edition published 1995 by
GLOBAL BOOKS LTD
PO Box 219, Folkestone, Kent, England CT20 3LZ

Third Edition 2000

© Global Books Ltd 2000

ISBN 1–86034–041–5

British Library Cataloguing in Publication Data
A CIP catalogue entry for this book
is available from the British Library

Set in Futura 11 on 12 pt by Bookman, Hayes, Middlesex
Printed in Malta by Interprint Ltd.

Contents

Foreword   7   Map of Russia   9

1 A Sense of History *10*
- A Brief History   *11*
- Westernization   *13*
- Revolution   *15*

2 The New Russia   *17*
- Problems of the 'New Abroad'   *18*
- Challenge of the Market Economy   *21*
- People and Poverty   *24*
- Changing Value System   *26*
- Entertainment   *28*
- Consumer Goods   *28*
- Political Melting Pot   *30*

3 The Russian People   *31*
- Family Life   *33*
- Failure of Socialism   *36*
- The New Super Rich   *37*

4 Travelling to Russia   *39*
- The Visa Challenge   *39*
- Arriving in Russia   *40*
- Go Where You Like   *43*

5 Hotels & Food   *45*
- 'Floor Ladies'   *46*
- Foreign Food   *48*
- Vodka Culture   *49*

6 Out & About   *50*
- Push Your Way In   *51*
- Two Types of Police   *52*

7 Shopping *53*
- The Queuing (Line-up) System *54*
- What to Buy *58*

8 Family & Way of Life *61*
- What is a Dacha? *63*
- Forms of Address *64*
- Friendship *65*
- Gift-giving and Home Visits *65*
- The Sporting Life *67*

9 Business in Russia *68*
- Trading Options *69*
- New Business Face of Russia *71*
- Official Holidays *73*
- Organizing Entertainment *77*
- 'Rebuilding' (*perestroika*) Reforms *78*
- Foreign Trade Reforms *78*

10 Russian Ways *80*
- Echoes of War *82*
- Weddings and the Church *83*
- Medical Matters *85*
- 'Open' Atmosphere *86*

11 Useful Words & Phrases *87*
- The Alphabet *87*
- Words & Phrases *88*
- Numbers *91*

Russian Words Used In This Book *92*

Facts About Russia *93*

Index *95*

Foreword

In 1991 the Soviet Union collapsed and it seemed possible that a new dawn could emerge for Russia. Now, nearly ten years on, writing about Russia at the end of the century is much more difficult than one might have imagined, because the situation can change very quickly, and often does!

For one thing, the priorities of some people in Russian society have changed: previously, in the former Soviet Union, education was prized very highly whereas today, although intellectuals still value education, the idea of making money as a primary objective is now very prevalent, particularly among the young.

Russia has never had a democratic tradition in the way that Britain, France or the United States have, and therefore trying to forge a democracy in Russia today is fraught with difficulties. Whether there will ever be democracy in the Western sense, it is impossible to tell, but many people are struggling to give Russia a future, while others are corrupt and line their own pockets. The poor in Russia today have a very difficult time and have to put up with a great deal of hardship and suffering.

Russia is not helped by many in the international media who do not seem to want to understand Russia's problems. There is a strong tendency to concentrate on crime and how dangerous Moscow and St Petersburg have become. True, there is more crime today than 25 years ago but no more than any other large city, e.g. London, Paris or New York. Of course, there is a mafia and organized crime does exist but this, on the whole, does not affect the person in the street, or tourists, or businessmen.

It is often said that Russia is paranoid about NATO and her borders. It is very important to remember, however, that these very borders have been under threat for centuries and Russia has always felt the need to defend them from attack even up to the present day. There is a sizeable minority in Russia who still perceive a threat to their motherland from the West. This is why Russia worries about NATO's expansion up to her frontiers.

It is very sad and difficult to watch a great country like Russia struggle to find itself in our modern world. But find herself she surely will one day. Russia is a wonderful, remarkable, frustrating place, with a really friendly people, and I only hope that the visitor to Russia will get to know, understand and love Russia and the Russia nation, as people have done in the past and will do so in the future, and not judge the country simply by the obvious criteria of just what is staring them in the face. It is very important to look behind the facade and try to understand what is really going on.

I.S.
November 1999

Map of Russia

1

A Sense of History

Moscow – the old and the new

Until 1991, Russia was the largest republic in the Soviet Union, and its influence can be felt even among those neighbours which try to pretend that they were never linked or that Russia no longer exists: they, too, must try to get along with their powerful neighbour. The Russian language is still the principal medium for communication, not only between Russia and former USSR republics, but also between non-Russian former USSR republics.

In 1995 the population of Russia was 148 million of whom 20% were non-Russians, involving 130 ethnic groups. There are nine time zones in Russia. The climate, as you would expect, varies enormously, from the extremely cold Arctic areas to the continental climate of the rest of Russia, with its extremes of hot and cold, to the temperate climate of areas like the Black Sea coast, Russia's 'Mediterranean' sea-side region.

It goes without saying, therefore, that if you travel to Russia in winter you should take a warm coat, gloves, boots and hat (preferably one with ear protection). For the other seasons, take the clothes you would normally expect to wear at these times in Western Europe or the eastern seaboard of the USA.

Hot Tip: Siberia's Huge Freshwater Lake

Lake Baikal in Siberia is the largest freshwater lake in the world. Its total area is 33,000 square miles and its maximum depth is 2122 feet. Some animal and plant species living in and around the lake are unique to it. Because of this, the lake is of immense interest to scientists.

A BRIEF HISTORY

The Soviet Union came into existence in 1922, after the Bolshevik Revolution of October 1917 and following the Russian Civil War. The revolution came about because of a complex set of circumstances. Briefly, the story up to 1917 is as follows:

In the tenth, eleventh and twelfth centuries AD, the region was divided into city states dominated by Kiev and known as Kievan Rus. These states were governed according to detailed codes of law and were as sophisticated as any in France and England at the time.

The story of Alexander Nevsky

In the first half of the thirteenth century, the Mongols (or Tartars, as they are sometimes known) conquered Russia. They did not occupy the territory, but insisted on maintaining disunity and levying heavy tribute from the Russian princes. This period of control, known as the Mongol Yoke, lasted roughly two-and-a-half centuries, until near the end of the fifteenth century, during which time Russia was cut off from developments in Europe, including the Renaissance. Moreover, Mongol influence continued to be felt in Russia for a long time after the yoke ceased.

The Mongol Yoke was finally lifted by the reunited Russian princes, under the Grand Duke of Moscow, Ivan III ('the Great'), but the Muscovite political system of centralized autocracy, supported by enforced religious Orthodoxy and a tightening knot of serfdom around the lives of ordinary people, showed clearly the imprint of oriental customs: in order to defeat the Mongols, Muscovy had, for the most part, come to resemble them. Isolation from the West was now gradually overcome as, first the British and then other Westerners, came to Muscovy to trade and establish other relationships as well. Ivan IV ('the Terrible') was even contemplating marrying the British Queen Elizabeth I.

WESTERNIZATION

Westernization started in earnest with Peter the Great, who reigned from 1689 to 1725 and spent part of his youth living in England as an apprentice. He forcibly 'dragged' Russia into the then modern world by reforming his court and the government system, establishing an 'arms-length' relationship with the Orthodox church, bringing women out of their semi-oriental seclusion, inviting the participation of Western architects, designers and mercenaries, setting up major state enterprises such as ship-building in the capital (which he also built, at the cost of thousands of lives) at St Petersburg and even forbidding the wearing of beards and kaftans.

To Westernize Russia, as the country was now known, Peter had to resort to Muscovite methods. Catherine the Great, who reigned from 1762 to 1796, continued this policy, reforming Russia by giving her nobles a greater share of power until the French Revolution of 1789 made her turn her back on Western ideas of change.

In fact, revolutionary ideas in Russia began to grow only after 1815, and made slow progress – at least at first.

Hot Tip: Literary Criticism!

Censorship was severe in nineteenth-century Russia, although a number of classic authors – Pushkin, Lermontov, Gogol, Turgenev, Tolstoy, Dostoevsky, Chekhov, Gorky, etc. – found ways to express their criticisms of the Tsarist system indirectly in their works.

Serfdom was finally abolished in 1861, but failed to improve the standard of living of the 90% of the population who were peasants: their protest, widely dispersed but deeply felt, continued to rumble on until the late 1920s.

After a national uprising in 1905, autocratic rule was modified by the addition of a legislative assembly, the State Duma. However, this lacked real power and became a forum for liberal criticism of the system. Only the Russian economy showed significant development at the end of the Tsarist period. In the years before the First World War Russian industry was growing at a very fast rate attracting large numbers of foreign investors. Russian workers grew in numbers, but continued to live lives of deprivation even by comparison with workers elsewhere in Europe. They had little influence over their lives and their misery translated directly into support for revolution. With little political support among the population, Tsarist Russia was now a giant with feet of clay.

Russian dolls

REVOLUTION

The advent of the First World War brought a temporary reconciliation with the regime, as it did in other countries. But before long, miserable conditions for the majority and evidence of incompetence at the top, amounting to betrayal in the pursuit of war aims, stripped away much of that loyalty. Soldiers – 'peasants in uniform' – began to desert *en masse* from the front, workers in the all-important heavy industries came out on strike and the Duma also uttered its public criticisms of the leadership. In 1917, two revolutions did away with the old system: the February Revolution toppled the Tsarist system and established a liberal Provisional Government in its place. This slowly slid to the left reflecting, though not adequately or in time, the public's mood. Then, in October, came the Bolshevik Revolution which established a Marxist government led by Lenin.

Hot Tip: When the Russian Calendar Changed

The Russian calendar was changed after 1917 to align Russia with the West: hence, the February Revolution actually took place in March, and the October Revolution in November!

Thus, when you go to Russia and try to understand what is happening today, it is vital to remember the country's history and the important part which that history has played and continues to play in the structure and development of modern life, perhaps even more important today when Russia is once again evolving and many aspects of life that were taken for granted no longer can be.

Hot Tip: Revolution Could Have Been Avoided!

If Nicholas II had introduced even limited democracy after the 1905 revolution, the Bolshevik Revolution of 1917 might never have taken place.

2

The New Russia

'Near abroad' countries

The situation in Russia has changed enormously in the course of the last few years, and is still changing. One of the most complicated and difficult areas of change is in the relationship between Russia and the newly independent states that made up the former Soviet Union. Russia used to be the most powerful republic in the USSR

(Union of Soviet Socialist Republics), and is now still the most powerful state in the Eurasian region. The Russians refer to this region as 'the near abroad' and, along with independence, a multitude of problems has arisen.

PROBLEMS OF THE 'NEAR ABROAD'

One such problem is the number of Russians living in the 'near abroad', e.g., the Baltic, Ukraine or Central Asia. In one of the Baltic states, Latvia, for example, Russians make up 46% of the population, and the nationalist Latvian government has to take this into account when making laws on citizenship. Estonia and Lithuania, the other new Baltic republics, have lower proportions of Russians, but even so they form a large ethnic minority in both countries, which has given rise to difficulties. These problems have not yet been resolved.

In the Ukraine, which is a Slav country with a language closely related to Russian and has been bound to Russia historically for over 300 years, Russians whose only home is in the Ukraine find themselves discriminated against, for example, with regard to employment, because they are not ethnically Ukrainian. Yet these people have nowhere else to go which they can call home. Similar things have been happening to Russians in the Central Asian republics, although here, it is true to say that historical ties are relatively recent and linguistic and ethnic links are lacking.

Hot Tip: The Problem of 'Near Abroad' Russians

If Russians living in the 'near abroad' were to be relegated to being second-class citizens, or subjected to direct persecution for their ethnic origins, the Russian government, which has publicly committed itself not to act as an imperial nation in these areas any more, would nonetheless find itself under great pressure from Russian public opinion, itself not unacquainted with nationalism, to intervene, perhaps even militarily.

Another aspect of the 'near abroad' problem is economic. When these areas were part of the USSR, they received deliveries of raw materials like oil and gas from Russia at subsidized prices which had not varied for years. Now Russia has to sell her oil and gas, say to Estonia, at world market prices, which Estonia is in no position to pay. As a result, Estonia has power cuts and no hot water for weeks on end. This fact does not improve relations between Estonians and Russians living in Estonia.

Changing the guard at Lenin's tomb, Moscow

Foreigners wishing to visit the 'near abroad' should telephone their appropriate embassies to find out if they need a visa to do so. Railway and air communications between Russia and the 'near abroad' are still intact and, though they will cost you hard currency, you can use them freely. On the whole, these countries seem to have settled for a regime where Russians need a visa to visit them, but Westerners do not.

The 'near abroad' problems also have a political dimension. In some of the countries on Russia's periphery, civil wars or other struggles for power are going on. Often, one faction is supported by Russia while the other is not. Very often, therefore, Russian troops are involved in keeping the peace or actively fighting on one of the sides. Examples of this are Tadzhikistan and Moldova. In most of these areas, civil strife has not reached such a pitch yet, but it could do. Additionally, there are parts of the Russian Republic where resistance to the Russian government has reached the level of armed struggle, e.g. in the North Caucasus.

Chechnya is the most recent problem. This, too, is part of the Russian Federation, but some elements in Chechnya would like to break away from Russia and form a Muslim fundamentalist independent state there. The Russian government opposes this for two reasons. Firstly, they argue that Chechnya is part of Russia and if they agree to its independence than other regions may decide that they do not wish to be part of Russia, thus creating a domino effect. Secondly, they do not want a Muslim fundamentalist state so close, especially as so many fundamentalists from Afghanistan, Pakistan and Iran are involved in the fighting, and therefore they have to make sure that this does not happen.

CHALLENGE OF THE MARKET ECONOMY

Russia is now struggling to become a capitalist democracy, and the change has brought many problems. Economic structures that were accepted as the norm in the USSR have largely disappeared, leaving many people confused and bewildered. The housing issue is a good example of this. Most flats in Russia belonged to the local councils.

With the advent of market conditions and in order to solve their own economic problems, the councils in many cases have decided to sell off their housing stock, offering it first to the sitting tenants. If these people can afford to buy, all well and good: if not, the flats are sold on the open market to whoever has the cash. In many cases, landlords have bought the flats putting the formerly subsidized rents up to 'market' (i.e. at much higher) levels. Many tenants, especially pensioners, have not been able to afford the new rents and have been evicted from flats which they occupied for decades, and, in the worst cases, have to live on the streets. The appropriate laws to safeguard individuals in such cases simply do not exist. Similarly, the poorly paid or unemployed have been hard hit, and cases of abandoned children have been known.

The street population in Russia's main cities has soared, bringing with it the familiar problems of begging, prostitution and mugging. This has all been reported in the Western press at great length, sometimes virtually monopolizing the coverage about Russia, thereby giving people the impression that Russia is a dangerous place compared to the West. It is true that the danger has increased by comparison with Russia as it was, say, ten years ago: but street danger has also increased in the West during this period.

Hot Tip: Using Good Sense to Avoid Danger

If you take the same precautions in Russia as you would in your own country, you should be perfectly safe: for example, do not walk around in very bright, expensive-looking clothes, do not stand around talking loudly in your own language and attracting attention to yourself, and do not go out even if you are only mildly intoxicated. On the other hand, do carry money in a bumbag or wallet close to your body and do not flash hard currency around.

Two Russian types

There are also problems with industry which used to be heavily subsidized. Many subsidies have in fact been retained under the new government, after an initial period of 'shock therapy' which left many enterprises in great difficulties. The political decision was taken to maintain employment and industrial power at the expense of doctrinal purity. Nonetheless, there are still many unemployed, and the problems of industry have shifted to another level: the need for large investment to modernize factories and their equipment.

The lack of a legal infrastructure for business leads to further problems: fraud is only one of them. Recently, there was the case of MMM, an investment firm which accepted money and privatization vouchers from the public, promising to pay very high interest rates on these investments and using a very slick Western-style advertising campaign in the media to attract savers. The firm went bankrupt, and thousands of small investors lost their money. There were no legal safeguards to protect the rights of those involved, many of whom were ruined financially.

PEOPLE AND POVERTY

In August 1998 President Yeltsin sacked his whole government and the rouble went into free fall, creating panic not only in Russia but in the West as well. Millions of Russians were affected by this and effectively the rouble was devalued, wiping out people's savings and buying power. This had a devastating effect on ordinary people and the economy, as many of them cannot afford things that they used to be able to afford, even some basic items like meat are often beyond the reach of a lot of people because they are now too expensive.

At the same time many workers were not getting paid for their work. People were not paid for months at a time in the state industries, and it is hard to imagine how some of them could manage. Many teachers, workers in factories, miners etc. have to have two jobs in order to maintain even a basic standard of living. A teacher would work all day in an institute and then in the evening give private lessons to the children of the 'New Russians' or work in a private school. It is amazing that people go to work even when they are not paid.

The expression 'after August 1998' has come into existence to mean that things have got worse. In the English-language *St Petersburg Times* for Tuesday 1 June 1999, there was a report of a poll taken about the economy, conducted right across Russia. In it 88% of Russians said that they feel the economy is in desperate straits and that there is no hope of a stable economy in the near future and things will only get worse. The poll also showed that young Russians are more hopeful: a senior executive at A.C. Neilson in Moscow said: 'Young Russians don't believe that a country so rich in physical and human resources can remain for long in this current state.'

Hot Tip: The 'New Value' Rouble

In 1999, the Russian government changed the rouble by taking off the last two zeros. The amounts of money had become far too unwieldy when £1 was 2,600 roubles or one dollar 2,100 roubles so it is now much easier for visitors to Russia when the rouble is worth 25 to the dollar or 34 to the pound.

From a sociological perspective, there is an interesting question to study. That is the mystery of the missing middle class. Under the new type of Russian capitalism, the old professional class that used to be the middle class has become so impoverished that it has ceased to be a middle class and there is nothing to put in its place. So there is no real middle class in the Western sense and the 'New Russians', i.e. the rich Russians who have holidays in the West, drive large four-wheel-drive cars, wear expensive Western designer clothes and live in a way that ordinary people can only dream of. Until a middle class comes back into existence, the structure of Russian society will not be adjusted properly.

However, life in Russia is not an unrelieved sea of troubles: city transport still works, people still go to work, children still go to school, students still attend colleges and universities, life goes on. It is simply that there are many new and unfamiliar problems which ordinary Russians are having to learn how to deal with.

CHANGING VALUE SYSTEM

Many traditional attitudes in Russia have changed (sadly). Education and intellectual achievement, for example, used to be regarded as important: now, it is financial and not educational achievement which is seen as more important – chasing the fast buck. In order to raise the standard of living, many people try to run their own business as well as working at their own paid job. Some people have even been able to concentrate entirely on the single objective of making money, creating a new class – the 'new rich'. It is said that there are around forty dollar billionaires in Moscow alone. These people drive fast foreign cars and have large mansions built for them outside Moscow or St Petersburg.

The new attitude has created a climate in favour of privatization. Many of the top state schools have already begun charging parents fees for their offspring's exclusive education. Similarly, in medicine, many doctors and dentists have gone over entirely to private work.

First day at school

Subsidies also supported 'cultural goods'. Books, for example, were very cheap before 1992, with large circulation figures. It was not unusual to see ordinary people on the Metro or buses reading the classics of Russian or European literature. Now, however, books are published at 'market-level' prices, in much smaller editions, much smaller numbers and much higher prices. The nature of what is published has also changed: in place of the classics, large editions are now devoted to the adventures of Angélique, Nat Pinkerton and other heroes of 'pop culture'.

ENTERTAINMENT

Theatres, too, used to enjoy subsidies and now no longer do in sufficient quantity. They are forced to seek money elsewhere, and although for the famous establishments, like the Moscow Bolshoi, it is less of a problem – by touring they can make large amounts of hard currency – for the smaller or lesser known theatres it is a hard battle for survival.

The Russian film industry faces similar problems: it has had to curtail production considerably, participate in many co-productions with companies from abroad and pay attention to a home audience which seems, if what was on in Russian cinemas in 1999 is any guide, to require films with a high sex and violence content and minimal intellect. Many Russians seem to have acquired the attitude (very quickly indeed) that whatever is home-produced cannot be interesting or worthwhile compared with Western productions which are correspondingly seen as important and interesting.

CONSUMER GOODS

This attitude also extends to consumer goods. Clothes with famous Western labels sell well, often to the 'new rich' and others who can afford the high prices; however, the prejudice described extends to those who cannot afford the prices but still look down on Russian goods. Foreign vodkas are advertised throughout Russia, and are on sale at prices several times those of the Russian product. Although Russian vodkas have always been of high quality, and are now considerably cheaper than the foreign product, they are beginning to sell less well than previously.

. . .advertisements for foreign brands'

Foreign ice-cream firms have moved their products onto the Russian streets, charging high prices, while traditional, good quality Russian ice-cream is both available and cheap. The media, especially TV, are no doubt mainly responsible for this change. Russian TV is now full of advertisements for foreign brands of items such as cat food or chocolate bars. Russians, too, are beginning to want these things. Russian TV has also changed in other ways. Now, soaps and game shows are commonplace. Not all changes here have been negative in their effects, however. High quality film and drama productions still take place, and in addition, investigative journalism has really taken off, followed with great interest by a public eager to see the source of misdeeds and corruption uncovered.

POLITICAL MELTING POT

Russia today is a political melting pot. There are many political parties from extreme right to extreme left. Each has its own party line, but none apart from the Communist parties has any long experience of political life and seems to have little taste for working together. There is a strong public desire for positive leadership, law and order and a stable economy and society. This has led to the growth of extremes: those who see the past as the model, the closet Brezhnevites, and those who look to extreme nationalism as Russia's salvation. Often the two extremes find that they have much to gain by cooperating, while politicians like the extreme nationalist Vladimir Zhirinovsky flourish, by promising those who are naïve enough to believe him that he will find a husband for every woman who wishes to marry, and attract a protest vote against President Yeltsin.

A study of Russian history shows that democracy did not establish itself there before or after 1917; with most of its prerequisites absent, it is inevitably now very difficult, therefore, to set up democratic processes throughout the country. Even President Yeltsin, democratically elected though he was, has not always acted in a democratic way, ruling by presidential decree which gives him very considerable personal power but without the sanction of parliament or public opinion.

Clearly, it will take a great many years for Russia to become a modern capitalist democracy with all the necessary infrastructures to protect the poor and needy as well as the rich and powerful. However, it is clear that the will is now present to achieve this eventually. Meanwhile, Russia is still an interesting and exciting place to visit and get to know, where the visitor can experience a real sense of history in the making.

Hot Tip: Russia is Still a 'Cash Society'

Most Russian people are paid in cash, and do not have bank accounts. Nor do most of them have credit cards yet, although this is likely to change in the future.

3

The Russian People

Three generations for dinner

The Russian people are as similar and as different as other peoples. They are similar in that, like everyone else, they all want to live well, bring up their children in peace, have fun, go on holiday, and work at something they enjoy.

The Russians are a Slav people accounting for over 80% of the Russian Federation. On the other hand, over the centuries there has been considerable intermarriage with minority peoples. Russian culture, however, has always enjoyed a dominant position, sometimes because that was the government's policy, sometimes because of the numerical predominance of Russians.

Russians are very proud of their country and heritage. Love of homeland is a very strong sentiment, as shown by the many patriotic songs and poems. Indeed, Russians are not ashamed to wear their love of country on their sleeves. After all, millions of Russians died in two world wars to protect their homeland, and the emotions which inspired past generations are very much alive, even in today's confused environment of rapid change.

Russians are a very hospitable, friendly and generous people. Visitors to Russia should try to make friends with individual Russians which should not be too difficult. There is widespread curiosity about foreigners and visitors who socialize with Russians should not be surprised to be invited home, where, often enough, they will be feted with a magnificent 'banquet'! Russians greatly enjoy and treasure friendship.

Enjoying winter sports (ski marathon)

To relax, like people the world over, Russians meet friends, go to restaurants, the cinema, the theatre and concerts. In winter they enjoy winter sports (e.g. skating, skiing), while in summer when the weather is good they go for walks in the city streets or, at weekends, to the country where many of them have a place to stay (the well-known *dacha*).

The *dacha* (see also pages 37 & 63) may be a whole house, or it may be a rented room or two in someone else's house: at all events, Russians will try to spend as much time as possible at there in the summer. Children may spend the whole summer holiday at the *dacha* with grandparents, while the parents visit at weekends. (It is commonly thought that it is better for children to spend the summer in healthy country air than in the stuffy city.)

FAMILY LIFE

These days, families have just one child. This is mainly because many women have a full-time job and, although child-care facilities exist, they are not available in all factories and neighbourhoods. It is also a fact that, in general, Russian men do not help much in the house, the burden of housework and child-rearing falling largely on the womenfolk. Russian apartments are small by Western standards.

Although in the constitution women were granted equality in pay and work (which they still have), they are not equal to men in society. This is slowly changing and there are the 'new men' who look after their children and help in the house. On the whole, this is the job of women, and is one of the reasons for having just one child, since it is usually the woman who helps her child with homework, cooks, shops, cleans and washes as well as working outside the home.

Another reason is that maternity services are still poor and women often have a very difficult time in childbirth with poor provision for pain relief and support. Men are not allowed to be with their wives and do not see their wives and children for a week or so after the birth. They can stand outside the hospital and shout up at them through the windows. The reason for this is that it is thought that they will bring germs into a clean environment.

Usually, a set of grandparents lives with a couple and child. There are various reasons for this. Firstly, it is unheard of to put a parent into an old people's home. Where these exist, they are usually awful, but families are close and support one another. Therefore, the grandparents will live with their children and help with the grandchildren, very often taking some of the burden of childcare from a young working mother.

The Russian male attitude to women has its roots in history. Up to 1861, people were physically owned by serf owners who could do what they liked with their serfs and therefore men thought that there was nothing wrong with owning your wife and beating her if you thought that she deserved it. It is very hard to abolish these attitudes even in today's climate. There are jokes such as:

'A dog is wiser than a woman, he won't bark at his master'; or
'A wife isn't a jug, she won't crack if you hit her'.

Hot Tip: Traditional Male Dominance is Still Accepted

Working-class women still accept that hard drinking and abuse is the norm and that a man not behaving in this way is not much of a man. It must be said, however, that these attitudes are slowly changing and women are learning that they do not have to put up with this sort of behaviour. There are many women, i.e. the impoverished professionals, who do not have to put up with these sorts of conditions and are slowly making sure that this is not the norm any more.

Divorce rates are currently the highest in the world (followed closely by the USA), with mothers mostly getting custody of the children: women with just one child find it easier to manage under these circumstances. Children continue to be regarded as very important in Russian society, are looked after as well as circumstances permit, and remain the centre of the still common three-generation family household.

Brown bears

FAILURE OF SOCIALISM

Today, many Russians are seeking something to give their lives new meaning. Socialism and Communism on Soviet lines seem to have failed and religion does not appeal to the majority. Nonetheless, in the new Russia, churches are open and functioning to a degree that was not tolerated until the mid-1980s. (Even before this, the Russian Orthodox Church always managed to coexist with the Soviet government.) The majority of church-goers are old people, although there are now also younger worshippers and the baptism ceremony has become increasingly popular.

Russian Orthodox church

In addition to religion, some people also turn to mystics, fortune-tellers and the so-called 'psychotherapeutics' who appear on television and effect 'cures' among their audience or at long distance. Even educated Russians at times can feel that their salvation lies in this direction, although this often leads to disillusionment when the so-called prophets are shown to be frauds and tricksters.

The class system in Russian society has changed little. There is still a large working class and a dwindling but still numerous peasantry. There is also a substantial intellectual class – an intelligentsia, which has now become poor – a legacy from the Soviet Communist era with its high value on education.

THE NEW 'SUPER RICH'

Hot Tip: The Danger of Being One of Russia's 'Super Rich'

In post-Communist Russia, a new élite of super-rich managers and businessmen have energed. They can be seen driving around in German cars with bodyguards, for the risk of doing business in Russia now is that making a killing on the market can have a literal as well as a metaphorical meaning.

The super-rich are also having vast mansion-like *dachas* built for them in the countryside around Russia's large cities. Ironically, many of the super-rich were members of the political and party élite during the Soviet period. The peasantry also have increased opportunities in the new Russia: by owning their land and producing for the market, they, too, can increase their wealth.

Unfortunately, however, a new very visible underclass has emerged in the new Russia: they are the dispossessed, people of all ages who have nowhere to live but the streets and public buildings, no skill but their ability to beg and no riches but what they can get by their wits.

Hot Tip: No Women's Movement in Russia

In Russia, unlike other European countries, there has been no strong women's movement. In law, women are guaranteed equality in pay and conditions. This is written into the constitution. However, since in practice women do nearly all of the child-care and housework alongside their full-time jobs, conditions for women are changing only slowly.

4

Travelling to Russia

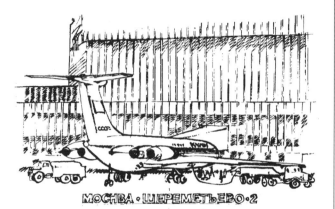

МОСНВА • ШЕРЕМЕТЬЕВО • 2

Sheremetyevo 2 Airport

THE VISA CHALLENGE

The most important prerequisite for anyone travelling to Russia is a visa which now has become even harder to get. Amazingly, it is more difficult to get a visa today than at the height of the Cold War.

For business and educational visas you will have to send a photocopy of the back page of your passport to the organization that is inviting or sponsoring you. This then will be taken by them to the Ministry of Foreign Affairs which after three weeks or so will issue an invitation which you need to send with the visa application form, passport, photographs, cheque and stamped addressed envelope. It is always necessary to have adequate travel insurance.

Your visa 'quest' would normally begin by applying to the Russian Consulate for a form, which can either be collected, sent in the mail or faxed. The form should be completed with great care and sent back with the required number of passport photographs together with your passport. The visa itself does not cost very much. It can take as little as a few days to process or as long as four weeks, or even longer. Allow time in your travel plans for organizing it.

ARRIVING IN RUSSIA

There are various ways to travel to Russia. Flying is the quickest way, but if you have more time it is worthwhile considering a train journey which from, say, the Hook of Holland to Moscow takes two-and-a-half days. There are also Russian ships which in Europe leave from Tilbury, Copenhagen, Stockholm or Helsinki; this is a very different sort of journey which can be very restful, interesting and a good introduction to Russian food.

On arrival in Russia, the traveller is issued with a customs declaration which should be filled in very carefully. On it are questions asking, for example, about how much money you are bringing into the country, whether you have illegal seeds or plants, guns or drugs, gold and jewellery on your person, or in your luggage.

You hand the form in to the customs officer on arrival, who usually stamps it as correct and hands it back to you. Keep it in a safe place, for you will need it on your exit from the country, when it will be compared with another form which you will fill in then.

Top Tip: Keep Good Accounts!

On leaving Russia, any discrepancies (e.g., taking out more money than you brought in) will result in lengthy questioning. The form was originally introduced to stop the illegal exchange of currency or goods, which used to be a problem. Nowadays, given that tourists are free – even encouraged – to use credit cards in restaurants, bars, banks, hotels etc., the form does not really keep tabs on how much travellers actually spend.

Young people travelling to Russia and staying for some time, may also be asked to produce a certificate testifying that they are free from AIDS.

Increasing numbers of people are now visiting Russia, either in groups or individually. There are also businessmen working more or less long-term out of Russia, and students studying there on educational exchanges or work placements.

If you simply want to 'discover' Russia, there are various options. You can go as an individual tourist, having a travel agent arrange for your travel, hotel, itinerary etc. This is usually a very expensive option.

St Basil's Cathedral, Red Square, Moscow

Alternatively, as most people do, you can go as a member of an organized group, where you pay a lump sum to the travel firm and everything is done for you. This is by far the easiest and most popular way to travel to Russia. Young people might like to tour Russia by car, camping as they go. It would be as well to ask your ministry of foreign affairs for advice about this option, as touring foreigners have been the object of criminal activities in the past. Also, you will have to submit an itinerary to the Russian Consulate for approval in advance of your receiving a visa.

> ## Hot Tip: Private Room Hire Now Available
>
> It is now possible to hire a room in someone's flat and also have meals with them. You will need a visa and you will have to register with the police on arrival. There are specialist agencies who make these arrangements.

GO WHERE YOU LIKE

Sometimes people travel to Russia with the impression that they will be supervised everywhere they go and only allowed where the authorities wish them to go, not where they wish to go. This is no longer true: these day visitors may break away from the group and wander at will. It is, of course, helpful if they can read and speak a few common phrases of Russian (see the Useful Words and Phrases at the back of this book). On the other hand, many Russians, especially the younger generations, speak European languages – English is the most common, but many speak German or French – and are very helpful to foreigners.

Trans-Siberian railway

Although officially you still need a visa mentioning each place you intend to visit, in practice no one will object if you have a visa for St Petersburg alone and decide to visit Moscow for the weekend.

Do not be dismayed if officials at airports and customs points seem unfriendly and unhelpful. Officials in such jobs are not noted for their welcoming friendliness anywhere. Individually, Russians are very relaxed and welcoming by nature. In fact, it is sometimes said inside Russia that hospitality is a Russian invention!

Alexander Column, St Petersburg

Hot Tip: There is More than One Kremlin!

Everyone knows that there is an outstanding building in Moscow called the Kremlin. But a kremlin is the word for a fortified city centre. Many Russian cities have ancient kremlins, e.g. Novgorod, Suzdal, Vladimir. Ancient Russian cities expanded outside their original kremlins only when the population got too big to live within them.

5

Hotels & Food

National Hotel & Intourist Hotel (right)

Having arrived in Russia and gone through the various formalities, you will be taken to your hotel. Quite simply, there are two types of hotel: old and new. The new hotels are usually very big and anonymous like similar hotels the world over. The older hotels, many of which in the big city centres are being modernized, have the most atmosphere and tend to be in good central locations.

The accommodation is usually in double rooms. Single rooms are more expensive. With your room key you will get a card or token with your name on it in Russian, and your room number. This is to enable you to get in and out of the hotel easily. Some hotels have introduced security guards at the doors, and you may be asked to produce proof of residence. If you do not speak Russian, you can also show the card to taxi drivers to get back to your hotel.

'FLOOR LADIES'

On each floor of the hotel there may be a desk by the lift or stairs occupied by a *dezhurnaya* (a woman charged with looking after the floor). These ladies used to report on what was going on to the authorities, but these days, in the spirit of *glasnost*, their function is obsolete: they are being phased out and you may find them very willing to talk with great curiosity and informativeness to foreigners – a potentially useful contact!

Registan Square, Samarkand

All large hotels have several restaurants, where the food is usually good and cheap and the service often slow (sometimes very slow). You can have a three-course meal with local wine for under £10 (US$15). Breakfast is normally available in a self-service restaurant in the hotel and is very substantial by Western standards – hot drinks, cheese, salami sausage, bread and soured milk or cream being supplemented by a whole hot dish, e.g. meat and vegetables. Russians often do not take lunch until late afternoon and need a large breakfast to sustain them in the meantime. Breakfast cereals are still a rarity. (The price for this kind of breakfast is around £2 ($3).)

Outside the hotel you will find speciality restaurants offering national dishes from Georgia, Armenia and other regions of the former USSR. These will be interesting for those who enjoy oriental cuisine and spicy foods. It is also worth exploring the wide range of Russian food: dishes like Chicken Kiev and Beef Stroganoff (a beef stew with cream) are well known, but there are many other dishes to try, including stuffed cabbage leaves, a range of very tasty soups and, what is less well known abroad, excellent cooked salads: ask for crab or *stolichnyi* salad and enjoy!

Hot Tip: Russians Love Their Food!

Russians love the pleasures of the table, and if you are lucky enough to be invited to a private home you will, almost certainly, find the table groaning with food, even in times of scarcity.

FOREIGN FOOD

Nowadays, in the large cities, restaurants serving foreign food are much easier to find. All the main 'chains' are represented: Macdonald's, Pizza Hut, Baskin-Robbins and numerous other familiar names serving fast food. Coca-cola is now available on the street or in restaurants. You will find Irish pubs, German bars, Chinese restaurants etc. in both Moscow and St Petersburg. Not unexpectedly, they are usually more expensive than outlets selling Russian food to Russians. If you can resist trying the familiar, you may find stalls on the street serving hot sandwiches and beer, home-made hamburgers or even wonderful *Pirozhki* (warm pies with meat or cabbage inside) or *Khachapuri* (hot unleavened bread with lumps of cheese inside). But check first to make sure hygiene precautions are being observed at kerbside stalls.

Kiosk in the Alexander Garden, Moscow ·

VODKA CULTURE

In the late 1980s, there was a campaign to discourage alcohol and reduce social and economic alcohol-related problems. This has now been abandoned and alcohol may be bought just about anywhere, from innumerable small kiosks on every main street and around most Metro (underground railway) stations. The enormous quantity of alcohol on sale – a bottle of vodka for under £4 (US$6) – means that much of it is of low quality, undrinkable or even poisonous. Buy a known brand from a shop, as Russians do. Be cautious about trying *samogon*, home-distilled vodka – it can be much stronger than official brands, containing 50% alcohol or more – and Russians swear by it as a cure-all. (See also p.28.)

Not all Russian drinks are alcohol-based. One delicious summer treat is *Kvas*, brewed from black bread and served from a tanker on the street or from a kiosk. *Kvas* tastes like a cool pleasant shandy and is very refreshing. Another summer treat is ice-cream served direct from portable freezers on the street. Russian ice-cream is well worth trying as it resembles the Italian product and is very cheap. You may also find a Russian ice-cream café selling champagne by the glass with its ices; an intriguing mix, and very popular with young Russians.

6

Out & About

Moscow Metro (Underground)

Public transport in Russia is cheap and reasonably efficient. The distances between cities are
generally so great that some people choose to fly
whenever possible. The long-distance trains, however, are comfortable, especially the 'soft' sleep-
ing accommodation. You are required to pay for
these fares in your own hard currency.

The underground (Metro) is found in most of
Russia's large cities. Stations can be recognized by the large red letter 'M' outside them,
even at night. The Metro is a well-maintained and

efficient service and stations are worth a visit just for the pleasure of it. The Moscow Metro, for instance, has a number of ornate and decorative stations, especially in the city centre. St Petersburg's Metro is more recent, and stations are correspondingly less ornate. Trains run every two minutes during the day and every five minutes in the evenings, up to 12.30 am or so.

PUSH YOUR WAY IN

Russians will push unceremoniously in order to get into a train, and accept being pushed with good humour on the whole. The fare is the same whatever the journey, the equivalent of less than 10p (US$20c.). For your money you get a counter (*zheton*), which you insert in a machine at the entrance to the escalators in each station. Using the Metro is straightforward if you read Russian: there are numerous notices in the stations and a map of the entire system in each carriage. On the other hand, you will find Russians quite willing to help a foreigner.

Buses, trams and trolleybuses tend to be far less frequent than the Metro and consequently packed, especially at peak periods. You buy a strip of tickets (they are even cheaper than the Metro *zhetons*) from the driver while the bus is still at the stop (or beforehand at kiosks on the street) and cancel one per journey at machines you will find in the buses.

Hot Tip: Be Extra Vigilant When Crossing the Road!

In big cities, main streets can be very broad and crossing the road can be quite difficult. Crossing places are marked out and crossing at an unmarked point or jay-walking can attract a small fine (to be paid on the spot) – and irate yells – from watching policemen.

TWO TYPES OF POLICE

There are two types of police whom the tourist will spot in Russia. First, there are the ordinary police, in royal blue uniforms and armed, like most police forces in the West: they are involved in the same sort of work as other police forces – such as traffic work and criminal investigations.

Second, there is the KGB, now known as the FSB. This organization has a fearsome reputation in the West. Under the Communist regime the KGB was a secret political police, with most of its operatives working in plain clothes. Since 1991, the KGB has opened up its files and its operations, which are now concerned with the fight against organized crime and the 'mafia'.* It is still a powerful organization, but the ordinary tourist or foreign businessman has nothing to fear from them any longer.

---

* The name may have changed but the organization is basically still the same.

7

Shopping

Currency

Money in Russia is made up of roubles and kopecks: 100 kopecks=1 rouble. In fact, inflation after 1991 rendered the kopeck obsolete and even individual roubles were worth almost nothing. Prices were counted in hundreds of roubles, and major Western currencies exchange officially for thousands. Since the change in currency after 1998 the Russians have gone back to roubles and kopecks.

You should take several forms of money with you to Russia: notes (US dollars are best, (a) because they are recognized everywhere, and (b) because they are available as notes on low denominations, unlike for example the British pound), traveller's cheques (American Express is most widely known, and even has branches in major cities, as well as refunding in case of loss or theft) and 'plastic money' (useful in an emergency at hotels, bars etc.).

You can change cash or traveller's cheques for roubles inside Russia but keep your receipts for these transactions as you may be asked to account for them at the customs when you leave. You are not allowed to take out of the country large amounts of roubles.

THE QUEUING (LINE-UP) SYSTEM

Shopping is time-consuming, not least because large supermarkets are less common than in the West. Most shops are small, specialize in a particular product range, and still feature queues ('lines' – though these are not as long as they once were). Rationing by shortage, which used to be universal, has been replaced by rationing by price. If you know that you cannot afford something, there is little point in queuing ('line-ups').

Out of habit many Russians still carry around in their pockets a string shopping bag known as an 'avoska' (from 'avos', on the off-chance). If they see something they fancy and can afford, they always have a bag to carry their purchase home in. Another old habit which has not died is the habit of joining a queue ('line') or crowd on the grounds that there must be something there for so many people to be interested in!

Take-away kiosks

Smaller shops tend to be somewhat old-fashioned. Packaging along Western lines is still not common, so you first queue to ask for your requirements, watch the shop-assistant measure out, wrap up, tell you how much and where to pay, then join a second queue at the cash-desk to pay your money and receive a paper receipt, and finally return to the counter to exchange your receipt for the goods which you have now bought.

It is to be hoped that this system will disappear in Russia just as it has disappeared in the West. You may be surprised to find the cashier using an abacus to calculate the total to pay: in the hands of an experienced operator, it seems to be as fast as a calculator however! Prices in rouble shops are generally quite cheap, and quality is sometimes not of the highest standard.

There are now also quite large supermarkets selling Western goods for roubles. In these shops you can find all sorts of groceries from

Kellogg's Cornflakes to Heinz Baked Beans There is Danish salami, Dutch and French cheese and various kinds of cold meat. There is of course Russian caviar which, although it is expensive for Russians, is cheap for foreigners owing to the favourable exchange rate.

These new shops are very modern and privately owned. What is interesting to see is that, while there are a lot of foreign foodstuffs on sale, there are few Russian ones, and it is necessary to ask where have the Russian sausage, salami, cheeses etc. gone.

Forming a queue ('line')

Large cities now have foreign currency grocery stores and supermarkets too, where you will find an even larger range of goods, usually aimed at foreign residents and at prices and quality similar to those in the West.

Walking about the streets of Moscow and St Petersburg, especially in the vicinity of Metro stations, you will be struck by the sight of hundreds of small kiosks, owned by the local council and let out to local traders selling anything and everything, from tea to tapes, from vodka to videos. Sometimes you can exchange hard currency for roubles at these places. Many well known Western brand names can be bought here, though the stock varies considerably from kiosk to kiosk, as do prices.

One of Moscow's best known department stores is the 'GUM' shop on Red Square. Formerly a British-owned store, it was nationalized during the revolution and has since 1991 been leased to private traders and foreign firms, e.g. Christian Dior. Inside GUM are three shopping arcades on three floors, which include seats and small cafés, and you, like many Muscovites, can spend many hours wandering around its warm, spacious interior.

Hot Tip: GUM: A Good Choice for Gifts

GUM is usually relatively cheap and has a comprehensive stock, so it is a good place to shop for souvenirs. Traditional Russian hand-painted wooden wares (plates, ladles, forks etc.) are examples of excellent and inexpensive presents.

A similar major store in St Petersburg is called 'Gostinyi dvor' ('Merchants' Courtyard') and is centrally situated on Nevsky Prospekt, the city's main artery. Here there is a branch of Littlewood's, the well-known British department store, where you can buy Western goods, e.g. breakfast cereal, for hard currency only.

GUM department store

WHAT TO BUY

There are many interesting and beautiful things to buy in Russia as souvenirs or presents. For example, amber and a wide range of semi-precious stones are made up into jewellery and sell cheaply by comparison with the West. Hand-painted wooden articles called 'khokhloma' make good gifts too. There is excellent porcelain from the Lomonosov factory in St Petersburg. Coffee-table art books are available at a fraction of the cost in the West, as are children's books translated into English. CDs, LPs and cassettes are also quite cheap. All these items are sold in shops and at stalls on the street – at stalls, you can even try haggling to reduce the price a bit.

Furs, on the other hand, have risen in price to Western levels so, unless you want to have a

Russian fur hat with a Russian label inside, this is no longer an essential tourist purchase in Russia. There is usually a good choice of articles in folk-woven materials, such as table-cloths, napkins, wall-hangings and highly decorative tea-cosies in the shape of dolls. Russian tea in enamel caddies, and electric samovars (the urn in which Russians heat water for tea and keep the teapot, with the brew in it, hot) also make excellent souvenirs or gifts.

Selling jewellery in the park

A visit to one of the many peasant markets is also worthwhile. Farm workers, smallholders and pensioners around the large cities grow for the urban market and bring their produce in to sell here. The bustle and the fragrance of the meat, dairy products, herbs, fruit and vegetables on sale, as well as the often unfamiliar varieties of mush-rooms, for example, make the peasant markets of great interest. Prices are usually higher than in shops, but the goods are often fresher (but let the buyer beware!) and more varied.

Ohe annoying custom lingering from the Soviet period is that of regularly closing establishments like shops and museums, with little warning, on pretexts like 'stocktaking day', 'shop cleaning day' etc. If possible, get someone to telephone ahead to ensure that the establishment is open when you wish to visit it.

Hot Tip: Best Buys in Jewellery

It is well worth buying amber jewellery or other semiprecious stones such as malachite. Such items are less than half the price they are in tthe West.

Town market

8

Family & Way of Life

Greetings!

Russian hospitality could well extend to a home visit invitation. However, if this is not offered do not take offence. It could well be that your Russian friend is embarrassed to take you into his/her home. It is well known that for decades there has been a real shortage of housing in cities, and much of what housing there is tends to be high-rise and cramped.

'Communal flats' (pre-revolutionary city-centre flats divided into single-room accommodation with shared kitchen, bath and toilet) are slowly being phased out, and there is an ongoing programme of building new flats on the outskirts.

Even so, many young people start married life sharing with his or her parents. Although it provides the couple with live-in babysitters, it means that already small flats are occupied, not by a nuclear family, but an extended family!

> ### Hot Tip: Shake Hands!
> Russians generally shake hands whenever they meet, much like the custom in France.

Living space used to be calculated as 11 square metres per person although now, with a virtually free market in property, you can inhabit what you can afford. This is little comfort in the inflationary conditions which have prevailed since the free market was introduced.

A 'shared kitchen'

Usually city-centre or suburban flats have from two-to-four rooms plus amenities. They are built in blocks around courtyards, often with play areas where the older people can sit while watching the children playing. Many flats are now being sold, either to individuals or to big businesses. Local councils which used to own the flats offered them to sitting tenants: if the tenants were unable to afford the price asked, the flats were sold to someone who could or rents were increased to 'market' levels. Tenants found themselves evicted from flats where they had lived for decades. This happened particularly to old people whose pensions have severely shrunk in value as a result of high inflation.

Hot Tip: How to Behave in a Russian Home

When you are invited to a Russian home, there are a few important rules of etiquette (although on the whole Russians are not as formal as Westerners once you get to know them). For instance, it is considered bad form to shake hands over the threshold. This belief has its roots in Russian folklore, where the threshold was considered to be the abode of the house spirit. Shake hands with your host only when inside the door.

WHAT IS A *DACHA*?

All around Moscow and St Petersburg you can see quality new country residences (*dachas*) under construction, commissioned by the new wealthy – the business élite. Usually, however, the *dacha* is a much humbler weekend residence, located just outside the city near a suburban train route, bought or rented from a villager. Here, vegetables are grown for family consumption or private sale, berries and mushrooms are collected in season and Russians spend a large part of their spare time at weekends and during the summer months relaxing from big-city pressures.

'Shake hands inside the door'

FORMS OF ADDRESS

The question of how to address someone can be quite perplexing. After 1917 the titles equivalent to 'Mr', 'Mrs', 'Miss' were abolished, to be replaced by titles like 'comrade' (*tovarishch*) and 'citizen' (*grazhdanin*). Now, the old titles, which before 1991 were used only ironically, are being revived again, though not yet in everyday speech.

When strangers meet, they will name themselves by their name, patronymic (a name, with both male and female forms, derived from the name of the father) and surname. Examples of these three names are Ivan Petrovich (the patronymic derived from Petr) Suslov and Natasha Petrovna (the female form) Suslova. The polite form of address is by first name and patronymic, but once you get to know people better you can agree to use their first name only. You may find that man and wife have different surnames: it is common in Russia for a married woman to continue to use her maiden name.

FRIENDSHIP

Russians are demonstrative people. Both men and women who are good friends will hug and kiss three times (on the cheeks only) when they meet a friend of the same sex, but it is less common for friends of different sexes to kiss on meeting. Friendship is expressed openly, like all emotions, in Russia. Men will walk hand in hand with one another, or arm in arm, as do women in both Russia and the West. There is no feeling that this behaviour is in any way homosexual: merely a public expression of mutual friendship.

GIFT-GIVING & HOME VISITS

When visiting a Russian home and going to see friends on returning home, it is very important to take presents. Russian people are very spontaneous and present-giving is a part of their way of life. It is essential, therefore, to make a gift plan before leaving. Russians would appreciate a picture of your local or native town, small items of clothing, good soap and books in a foreign language. For young people, cassettes of Western pop music are very welcome and if you want to be especially generous to someone who has been particularly helpful and kind, you could always give your Walkman as a leaving present; this would be very much appreciated!

Typical Russian 'zakuski'

Top Tip: Enjoy the Toasts but Watch the Vodka

Whether you go visiting in a private flat or hold an official dinner there will probably be toasts and speeches at the table. The meal begins with *zakuski* (hors d'œuvres), comprising various salads, salami sausage, cold fish, *pirozhki* etc., usually served with vodka.

Vodka is served in small glasses and should be drunk in one go, not sipped. Someone may propose a toast, everyone will drink their vodka and then eat some *zakuski*. On a ceremonial or formal occasion, there may be several toasts, so eating *zakuski* is an essential precaution.

Remember that vodka can have a swift and devastating effect on an empty stomach!

Typically, the Russian dinner table will be covered with various tasty dishes. It is important to try the food, so eat a little of each. If you do not like something, you need not touch it again. Russian champagne might also be served with the meal, or one of the quality Georgian wines. After the meal, you may be offered further drinks: various fruit liqueurs or vodkas, Armenian, Dagestan or Georgian brandy.

People usually remain sitting at the table after the meal is finished, enjoying an animated discussion until it is time to go home. At the end of the meal, tea and coffee are served, often accompanied by large and delicious cakes (*tort*), frequently elaborately prepared with cream and chocolate, and beautifully decorated.

THE SPORTING LIFE

Sport has always been encouraged in twentieth-century Russia, particularly in the period of the Soviet Union. Now Russia on her own has fewer resources but national teams are well supported. Football is very popular, with teams from all over the country competing in league matches.

There are many sporting opportunities available. The visitor might enjoy cross-country skiing and skating in winter, but you should bring your own boots. Every district has its own exercise class and people go to fitness centres to work out. Other popular sporting activities include riding, ice and field hockey, tennis and swimming. Many municipal swimming pools demand health certificates from Russian doctors before you are allowed to use them, but this does not apply to clubs.

9

Business in Russia

Russian offices are open from 9.00 am to 6.00 pm

Business people travelling to Russia will need an ordinary visa (as opposed to a tourist or transit visa). For this you will need the following:

1. A completed visa application form.
2. Three passport-type photographs
   (4 cm. × 4.5 cm.).
3. A valid passport.
4. A letter from your company or organization explaining the purpose and itinerary of your visit, the organization which you will visit in

Russia, the length of your stay and the flights which you propose to take there and back.

5. Most important of all, a letter, telex, telegram or fax from the Russian organization indicating that they know you and are expecting you. Without this you will not get your visa.

Transit visas are usually valid for only 24 hours, for travellers stopping over in Russia on their way to other destinations, such as Japan or India.

TRADING OPTIONS

If you wish to start trading in Russia, there are various ways to do this. Firstly, you should get in touch with the Russian Foreign Trade Ministry or, secondly, you should get in touch with the Russian Trade Mission wherever you live. You can get a business visa only through a trade mission or ministry sponsorship. You could exhibit your products at one of the exhibitions in Moscow or elsewhere, as these enable Russians to see foreign equipment and foreign products at first hand. Moscow's Expocentre is responsible for organizing exhibitions.

You can also start a joint venture or partnership with a Russian and import goods into Russia. For this you will find having a Russian partner very useful, if not essential, for he or she will know the ropes and be well motivated in ensuring the success of the venture. Foreigners are also permitted to own cafés, bars and restaurants, but again it is helpful to have a Russian partner.

Top Tip: When to Ring Top Officials

Russian offices are open from 9.00 am to 6.00 pm Monday to Friday. Try to arrange your appointments well in advance otherwise you may face delays. The best time to ring top officials is usually between 9.00 and 10.00 am.

It is advisable to send a telex or fax to each organization you intend to visit, telling them when you will come to see them and what you want to discuss with them; also, try to include a résumé in Russian, at least two weeks before your departure. The commercial department of your embassy can help to follow up these matters for you.

Hamburger enterprise

Nevertheless, it is so much better if you make your own appointments, as the Russians prefer this and are therefore more likely to look favourably on you. Most Russian firms have a telex or fax machine, but not all do. It might be better, therefore, to write to the organization with which you wish to have dealings. Remember, however, that letters can take up to two weeks to arrive.

If your company does not get a reply to its letter it might not mean a negative answer. It could depend on whether or not there is hard currency available for your product. Officials must have detailed information so that they can plan for funds to be allocated several years in advance. You will need, therefore, a great deal of patience, tolerance and perseverance, but you could be more than amply rewarded.

NEW BUSINESS FACE OF RUSSIA

There are many Western-style businesses in Russia today which have computers and therefore e-mail is quite commonly used. There are computer shops and people are very knowledgeable about the latest software. Answering machines, voice mail and faxes are far more common now than even five years ago.

It is interesting to see all the familiar Western firms doing business on Russian streets. Foreign businesses are a familiar sight now and no-one is surprised at the advertisements for Volvo cars, Ariston washing machines or Snickers ice-cream. Foreign cigarettes, drinks and all other goods are on regular sale everywhere.

On the streets it is possible to see advertisements for fitness centres and people going there to work out as in any other European country. There are many new business ventures and, while some go to the wall, others are successful.

In the newspapers there are advertisements for electrical and other repairers, painters and decorators etc. These firms are very busy, giving much-needed employment to the unemployed Russians.

Another aspect of emerging capitalism is the area of real estate. Firms compete with each other to provide the glossiest brochures advertising luxury offices and apartments in beautiful buildings in the centres of Moscow and St Petersburg. These firms offer a range of services from guarded parking to on-site management, 24-hour security to fitness centres – a controlled environment in which business people can relax and feel safe.

There are specially designed condominiums and executive-style housing with 24-hour security. Such foreign firms have moved into Russia and taken over whole areas, designing them for the foreign business person. There is even a firm called Pulford that offers the business person special flats, for long or short lease, with everything done, including shopping, washing, cooking and cleaning, instead of staying in a hotel.

These new business ventures, while good for the foreign firms, do not really bring prosperity to Russia as the money goes out of the country, and although cleaners, cooks and laundry staff do earn more money today it is not enough to help the economy.

Hot Tip: Take Enough Business Cards

Make sure that you have enough business cards with you – one side printed in English and one in Russian.

OFFICIAL HOLIDAYS IN RUSSIA

Orthodox Christmas	7 January
New Year's Day	1 & 2 January
Women's Day	8 March
International Labour Days	1 & 2 May
Victory Day	9 May
Birthday of St Petersburg	29 May
Anniversary of the Bolshevik Revolution	7 & 8 November
Constitution Day	12 December

If an official holiday falls on a Tuesday, then the preceding Monday is also declared a holiday but the following Saturday becomes a working day. August is the main holiday month, so it is advisable to avoid visiting Russia on business then. The first two weeks in May and the first two weeks of November can also be difficult; evidently these are periods when it is best to avoid making appointments.

Some firms still stick to the old holidays, but many do not, so it is best to find out in advance when they take their holidays. The Russian Orthodox Christmas is now celebrated again – it falls in the early part of January – so, what with the New Year it is advisable to avoid the first half of January altogether for business purposes.

Some of the holidays have changed in importance. Christmas and New Year form one long holiday and the anniversary of the Bolshevik Revolution on 7 November is no longer celebrated by an official military parade as it used to be. However, some other holidays are celebrated with great enjoyment. One of these is the birthday of the city of St Petersburg on 29 May. It is an amazing day, as it is also the start of the White Nights (see 'Facts About Russia' p.93). The White Nights of St Petersburg take place from the end of May to the beginning of July, and create a truly magical environment.

On the evening of 29 May, people pour into the main street of Nevsky Prospekt, an eight-lane highway, and march along singing and talking animatedly. So great is the crowd that, for safety reasons, several underground stations along the route are closed. The atmosphere is happy, relaxed and good-humoured.

If you wish to receive letters from your company while you are in Russia, it is advisable to get them sent to the commercial department of your embassy and collect them from there, having first advised your embassy that you will be doing so. This is because you are unlikely to know the name of your hotel before you leave. It is also possible to send urgent mail, including parcels, by courier.

Local telephone calls are free from your hotel and you can usually dial direct from your room. Sometimes you may have to go through the hotel switchboard, in which case ask for *górod* (city) and you will get a direct line.

You can also telephone from machines in the street. Because of inflation and the difficulty of finding change, you use a Metro counter as the coin in the slot. It is more convenient to ring from your hotel or from a friend's flat. Directories are rarely to be found, but all hotels have service bureaux which will find telephone numbers, addresses etc for you, and you will also see information kiosks on the street where, for a fee, you can obtain similar information.

There is now direct dialling to North America and most West European countries from St Petersburg and Moscow. You can order an international call from your hotel or make one from the main Moscow post office at 7 Tverskaya (Gorky) street. There are operators at the international exchange who speak most common foreign languages.

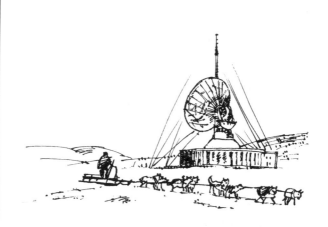

Russian communications in Siberia

If you urgently need more money, currency can be transferred to the Bank of External Economic Affairs (Vnesheconombank), Department of current accounts and transfers. The telex no. of Vnesheconombank is 411174 and the telephone number is (Moscow) 232-53-00.

There are also American Express representatives at 21a Sadovo-Kurenskaya Ulitsa (tel. (Moscow) 254-43-05) and at St Petersburg in the Hotel de l'Europe (just off the Nevsky Prospekt) who can help you. If you or your firm plan to be in Russia for some time you might want to have a Russian Savings Bank Account which can be used all over the country. This can also be arranged by Vnesheconombank. Currency exchange, purchasing and customs arrangements are the same for business people as for the ordinary tourist.

ORGANIZING ENTERTAINMENT

In carrying on your business, you may wish to host a dinner or reception. This can be arranged at certain hotels and restaurants, including Moscow's Mezhdunarodnaya Hotel. The hotels National and Metropole, in the centre of Moscow, can be used for small numbers: the Budapest Hotel has a large banqueting hall for big receptions. You can also use the foreign currency restaurants, e.g., in Moscow's Intourist, Kosmos, Metropole, Mezhdunarodnaya and National Hotels. There are also many bars which accept foreign currency.

You may need to hire a car with driver. You will pay less for a Russian car than for a foreign one, less for a small car than for a big one. Usually the charge is calculated for the first eight hours, and then for each hour after that. Prices vary considerably, particularly if you are paying in roubles, so shop around to find the best bargain to suit your requirements. There may be an additional charge if you go over 240 kilometres or if the driver works over ten hours.

Business people who have an international driving licence with details in Russian can also hire a self-drive Lada car, paying in addition for the cost of petrol and insurance. You will need to be familiar with traffic regulations, copies of which are available in a number of foreign languages. Street maps and plans can be bought in hotels, newspaper kiosks and bookshops.

Frozen north pipelines on pilings

'REBUILDING' ('*PERESTROIKA*') REFORMS

The Russian leadership since 1991 seems to have understood the need for drastic domestic change and has brought in numerous new economic freedoms which mean that enterprises can take charge of their own affairs, for example by allowing them to manage their own profit. *Perestroika* – rebuilding – changed many things in the areas of foreign trade and banking, and encouraged the establishment of new enterprises throughout Russia.

THE FOREIGN TRADE REFORMS ARE:

1. Foreign trade can be organized by many more Russian enterprises than previously.
2. Russian enterprises will have to have hard currency bank accounts. However, money coming into these accounts is subject to state and local taxation amounting to 69%. Ways of circumventing this include foreigners taking the cash into Russia personally.

3. There is a new ministry to help overseas trade.

4. There will be more encouragement for exports, marketing and joint ventures. Joint ventures have been possible since January 1989 on the basis of 51% Russian and 49% foreign participation. Westerners themselves can now open businesses in Russia, and the big multinationals have moved in quickly.

Russians are very keen to utilize Western know-how, especially in those areas where they lag behind. There are some points which are particularly important. (1) It is vital that the joint venture should produce enough to pay the Western partner. (2) It should replace something being imported already (3) It should show improved quality and bring new technology into Russia.

There are several areas where joint ventures are especially welcome: agro-industry; food processing, packaging and distribution; areas of high technology such as computers and digital machine tools; paper production; shoes and clothing; tourism; and advertising.

Hot Tip: Siberia's Fantastic Wealth

Siberia produces all the gold, ornaments and precious stones that Russia needs. It also contains vast quantities of oil, gas and coal. Russia even sells natural gas to Germany.

10

Russian Ways

St Petersburg

Many people have heard the story that there are no plugs in wash-hand basins in Russia. This is perfectly true. The point is, plugs are not provided, not because there is a shortage, but because Russians prefer to wash under running water believing it to be more hygienic. So, if you feel that you need a plug for hand-basins, buy one that adapts to different sizes of sink before you leave, and take it with you.

Generally speaking, lavatories are Western-style in Russia and are reasonable. Of course, they are perfectly alright in private flats and hotels and are usually well maintained in restaurants and bars.

It is sometimes possible, however, particularly away from the city centres, to find very primitive or poorly maintained facilities, perhaps little more than a hole in the ground or with little privacy. Sometimes, too, because of a shortage of toilet paper, you will be provided with the alternative of cut-up newspaper. If this sort of thing concerns you, carry some toilet paper around with you. Such primitive facilities are, however, becoming less common with the passage of time.

In winter, when people go out wearing layers of clothing, it is the custom to leave the outer layer – coat, boots, hat, scarf, gloves – in a cloakroom when you enter a public place, e.g., an office, theatre, restaurant, library. The cloakroom attendant will give you a token or ticket so that you can collect your clothes when you leave. In Russia, it is not customary to sit indoors in a heavy outdoor coat.

Going to the theatre in Russia is a very special occasion, and you will see people there dressed as if for a party. The intervals are longer than is general in the West, and people use them to walk around the theatre (often a magnificent old building), have a snack and/or drink at the buffet or meet friends and have a chat. Conversation is normally very lively, and theatres, operas and ballets are heavily booked throughout the year. Your hotel will be able to help with the purchase of tickets. Expect to pay for these in hard currency.

Prima Donna

You may be able to buy unwanted tickets, however, by standing outside the theatre building a half-hour or so before the performance and see if anyone is ready to sell one of theirs. (It is normal to offer the price of the seat, no more, and in roubles, in these cases.) The Russian circus is also worth a visit, being of a very high standard and considered in Russia as a performing art equal with the ballet.

ECHOES OF WAR

For Russians, even today, the events of the Second World War retain much more importance than in the West. There is scarcely a family that did not lose a friend or relative. The history of the war is taught in all the schools, and therefore everyone knows the essential facts. For example, they know that Leningrad* (St Petersburg) was under siege for 900 days and there are reminders of this in the sign on Nevsky Prospekt warning passers-by to walk on that side of the street during bombardments.

In every city there are war cemeteries and memorials which are a very moving sight, and it is possible that you may be taken to one of these. The cemetery on the outskirts of St Petersburg contains over a million war dead.

Most Westerners know little about Russia's sufferings during the Second World War, and therefore gaining some background knowledge before leaving would be worthwhile. Do not be surprised to see wedding parties at a war cemetery. It is still the custom for a just-married couple to go and lay flowers on one of the memorials and commemorate the dead.

Many parts of Russia were destroyed by the Nazis. However, since the war the Russians have spent a good deal of money and effort in restoring their historical past as you will see if you go to Peter the Great's palace at Petrodvorets or Catherine the Great's at Pavlovsk, both outside St Petersburg and beautifully restored after being severely damaged during the war.

WEDDINGS AND THE CHURCH

Weddings in Russia are celebrated with a certain amount of ceremony. Since most

---

* Leningrad was the name of the city of St Petersburg during the siege and therefore the name is retained when talking about that period. It is interesting to note, by the way, that while the city changed its name (after a referendum) in 1991, the region of which St Petersburg is the largest town is still called the Leningrad Region. The city was founded by Peter the Great in 1703. During the First World War its name changed to the more Slavonic-sounding Petrograd.

people want to mark the event, and at one time religion was the object of extreme official disapproval, the Soviets came up with the idea of the wedding palace. More than just a registry office, this is a place where the ceremony is conducted with a show of pomp. The bride wears a white dress, there is solemn music, flowers and photographs, and the building itself is decorated and furnished with a certain amount of luxury and show.

Nowadays, however, the Russian Orthodox Church has become almost an official state church, there are more working churches than there have been for years and anyone may participate in church services if they wish. The restoration of many churches is under way, often with state aid, and relations between church and state have improved enormously; church dignitaries have even entered the state *Duma*, the parliament, as deputies.

Sergiev monastery

MEDICAL MATTERS

Medical treatment in Russia is no longer free, as it used to be up to 1991. Expect to pay for any treatment you may be given, and equip yourself with medical insurance accordingly. Normally, treatment can be arranged for you by your hotel. There are no general practitioners as such, but generalist doctors who work at polyclinics and refer patients to specialists and/or hospitals as necessary.

Treatment for foreigners often takes place in hospitals reserved for them. If you know what medicine you require, you can often buy it at a chemist yourself: a wide range of medicaments is available over the counter without prescription.

There are many horror stories around about the current state of Russian medicine. It is true that there are shortages of medical items (ditto non-medical items) and if you are unfortunate enough to fall seriously ill in Russia, or have a bad accident, your insurance company may insist on your being returned home. But Russians are not dying in greater numbers from illnesses than they used to, so a few sensible precautions will see you all right.

Hot Tip: Bring Your Own Syringe!

If you are likely to need injections or tests, take a few disposable syringes with you: not only is there a shortage of this basic item, but your own supply reduces the risk of AIDS. If you are fortunate enough not to need them during your stay, they would make a prosaic but most acceptable present!

On the whole, letters and cards take about ten days to reach Western European countries and two weeks to reach America. If you are in Russia for a few weeks, therefore, it is quite possible to receive mail from abroad and reply to it. It is also possible for business people to send faxes and telexes quite freely and, with direct dialling in may areas, use of the telephone has become much easier.

'OPEN' ATMOSPHERE

Since the mid-1980s, with the Gorbachev period of *glasnost* and *perestroika*, most Russians are happy to talk freely about their conditions of life and make their views known even to foreigners. The new atmosphere of freedom of criticism is also reflected in the media, despite government attempts to rein it in a bit. The political scene has become very interesting, and sometimes threatening, as the Russian people learn to exercise their new democratic rights.

Hot Tip: 'The Good Old Brezhnev Days'!

You will find a surprising number of people nostalgic for the Brezhnev period – the twenty years or so before *perestroika* – when, according to them, life was calm and orderly, food was generally available and reasonably priced and you could anticipate what the next day would bring.

11

Useful Words & Phrases

THE ALPHABET

The Alphabet can be divided into three groups to make it easier to learn.

1. *Those letters that look like English and have English sounds.*

А а	a	bu**ck**
К к	k	**k**ite
О о	o	c**o**t
М м	m	**m**other

2. *Those letters which have English sounds, but look different.*

Б б	b	**b**rother
В в	v	**v**est
Г г	g	**g**ate
Д д	d	**d**oor
Е е	ye	**y**et
Л л	l	**L**ondon
З з	z	sei**z**e

И и	ee	f**ee**t
Н н	n	**n**ormal
П п	p	**p**aper
Р р	r	**r**adio
С с	s	**s**tove
Т т	t	**t**on
У у	oo	c**oo**l
Ф ф	f	**f**ather
Ц ц	ch	crun**ch**
Ш ш	sh	**sh**abby

3. *Those letters which have Russian sounds and look different.*

Ё ё	yo	**yo**ur
Ж ж	zh	mea**s**ure
Й й	is the **y** in the word to**y**	
Х х	kh/c	lo**ch**
Ц ц	ts/tz	fi**ts**
Щ щ	shch	fre**sh ch**eese
Ы ы	the nearest is the **i** in the word ill	
Э э	e	as in the word g**e**t
Ю ю	u	**u**niverse
Я я	ya	**ya**rd
Ъ ъ	hard sign	
Ь ь	soft sign	

WORDS & PHRASES

здравствуйте	zdrastvuytye	hello
доброе утро	dobroe ootro	good morning
добрый день	dobrii den	good day

добрый вечер	dobrii vecher	good evening
спокойной ночи	spokoynoi nochi	good night
меня зовут	menya zavoot	my name is
пожалуйста	pozhalooista	please
спасибо	spasibo	thank you
вокзал	vokzal	station
Метро	metro	metro/underground
станция (метро)	stantsiya (metro)	station (underground)
улица	ulitsa	street
проспект	prospekt	avenue
идите	idite	go
стойте	stoite	stop
переход	perekhod	pedestrian crossing
театр	teatr	theatre
кино	kino	cinema
концерт	kontzert	concert
цирк	tzirk	circus
музей	moozey	museum
завод	zavod	factory/plant
магазин	magazin	shop
вход	vkhod	entrance
выход	vikhod	exit
закрыто	zakrito	closed
касса	kassa	cash desk
телефон	telefon	telephone
почта	pochta	post office
банк	bank	bank
ремонт	remont	repairs
справочный стол	spravochnii stol	information desk
театральный стол	teatralnii stol	theatre desk
паспортный стол	pasportnii stol	registration desk

буюро обслуживания	byuro obsluzhi-vaniya	service bureau
сувениры	suveniri	souvenirs
гостиница	gostiniza	hotel
ресторан	restoran	restaurant
кафе	kafe	cafe
буфет	bufyet	buffet
чай с молоком	chai s molokom	tea with milk
чай с лимоном	chai s limonom	tea with lemon
кофе с молоком	kofe s molokom	coffee with milk
черный кофе	cherni kofe	black coffee
вино	vino	wine
пиво	pivo	beer
за ваше здоровье	za vashe zdorovye	to your health/cheers
было очень вкусно	bila ochin fkusno	it was delicious
я не говорю по-русски	ya ne gavaryu pa-russki	I do not speak Russian
аптека	apteka	chemist
больница	bolnitza	hospital
мне надо к врачу	mne nado k vrachoo	I need a doctor
не курить	ne kurit	no smoking
Москва	Moskva	Moscow
Ленинград	Leningrad	Leningrad
Ст петербург	St Peterburg	St Petersburg
Киев	Kiev	Kiev
Рига	Riga	Riga
Ереван	Yerivan	Erevan
Тбилиси	Tbilisi	Tbilisi
Таллин	Tallin	Tallinn

сколько стоит	skolko stoit	how much
один рубль	odin rouble	1 rouble
два рубля	dva roublya	2 roubles
три рубля	tri roublya	3 roubles
четыре рубля	chetire roublya	4 roubles
пять рублей	pyat roublyei	5 roubles
шесть рублей	shest roublyei	6 roubles
семь рублей	sem roublyei	7 roubles
восемь рублей	vosem roublyei	8 roubles
девять рублей	devyat roublyei	9 roubles
десять рублей	desyat roublyei	10 roubles
сто	sto	100

NUMBERS

тысяча	tisicha	1,000
пять тысяч	pyat tisich	5,000
десять тысяч	desyat tisich	10,000
пятнадцать тысяч	pyatnadtzatz tisich	15,000
двадцать тысяч	dvadtzatz tisich	20,000
тридцать тысяч	tridtzatz tisich	30,000
сорок тысяч	sorak tisich	40,000
пятьдесят тысяч	piddisyat tisich	50,000
шестьдесят тысяч	shestdisyat tisich	60,000
сто тысяч	sto tisich	100,000

Russian Words Used In This Book

авоська	avoska	string shopping bag
гласность	glasnost	openness
город	gorod	town
гостиный двор	gostiny dvor	*literally*, 'merchants' courtyard'; title of a big store in St Petersburg
гражданин	grazhdanin	citizen
ГУМ	GUM	title of the big store in Moscow
дача	dacha	country dwelling
дежурная	dezhurnaya	duty maid or concierge
жетон	zheton	token
закуски	'zakuski'	hors d'œuvres
овощи	ovoschi	vegetables
паспортиый контрол	pasportny kontrol	passport inspection
пирожки	pirozhki	little pies
перестройка	perestroika	reconstruction
проспект	prospekt	avenue
столичный	stolichny	capital (adjective): also name of a salad
товарищ	tovarisch	comrade
фрукты	frukty	fruit
хачапури	khachapuri	unleavened bread with cheese baked in it
хохлома	khokhloma	wooden painted crafts

Facts About Russia

In terms of land mass, with an area of 17,075,000 square miles, Russia is the largest country in the world: it is almost twice the size of China. It has a population of 148,000,000, 80% of which is ethnically Russian, the remaining 20% belonging to over thirty minority ethnic groups.

The White Nights in St Petersburg take place in June. It gets dark only at about 2 o'clock in the morning, and gets light again at around 5.30 in the morning. It is a wonderful time as it is usually warm by then and people walk around in the streets, just for the pleasure of being out until midnight or later.

Moscow has been the capital of Russia since the Bolshevik Revolution. Before that, St Petersburg was the country's capital and has many wonderful palaces that are well worth visiting.

State school education starts at seven years of age, but most children also go to nursery schools from an early age, where they learn to read and write. Education is compulsory until the age of sixteen.

In Russia, traffic drives on the right. The roads are often in bad repair and many of the distances are so great that people prefer to fly. There is a traffic police force which has police boxes in the main cities, often at crossroads, and they often stop traffic for random checks.

For the Russians, their culture is very important to them. Folk stories and songs describing the motherland are sung by everyone. Every child knows about Pushkin and can recite his poetry. Love of one's country is nothing to be ashamed of for Russians.

Most of Russia's great literature can be found in the nineteenth and twentieth centuries. There is very little written before the eighteen hundreds. The giants of Russian literature wrote in the nineteenth and early twentieth centuries.

In the palaces and museums, you will be given felt slippers to wear over your street shoes. This is to protect the floors which are made of very beautiful old wood. The trouble with these shoes is that they always fall off, sometimes the ties have broken, and they are not always the right size. It is quite a feat to walk in these.

Russian Orthodox

The official religion of Russia is Russian Orthodox which now attracts more people into its churches than for many years, though many of these are elderly.

In the Russian Orthodox religion, icons play an important part. These are typically images of saints or the Virgin Mary, and they are prayed to by worshippers who hope their prayers will be answered. Some old icons can be very valuable, even encrusted with precious stones and with a gold or silver cover.

The Russian bathhouse (*banya*) is a great experience. It is a bit like a sauna, but typically Russian. It is well worth trying. A client is given a bunch of twigs with which, after the steam bath, they gently hit their skin, which gives a great sense of well-being.

Some of the great museums (e.g., the Hermitage in St Petersburg, the Pushkin Museum in Moscow) have wonderful collections of great art like the former's Rembrandts and Impressionists. Do not miss the Tret'iakov Gallery in Moscow, with its unique collection of Russian art.

If you go to Russia in the winter, do go on a sleigh drawn by three horses (*troika*). It is an interesting experience to drive through the snow in one of these.

Index

Afghanistan 21
AIDS 41, 85
American Express 54
Alexander Column 44
Armenia 47

Baltic 18
Baskin Robbins 48
Bolshevik Revolution 11, 16, 74, 93
Bolshoi Theatre 27
Brezhnev 86

Catherine the Great 14
Catherine the Great's palace 83
Central Asia 16
Chechnya 20
Chekhov 14
Civil War 11
Coca Cola 48
Cold War 39
Communism 36
Communist Party 29
Copenhagen 40

Dacha 33, 37, 63
Dostoevsky 14
Duma 14, 84

Elizabeth I 13
Estonia 18, 19
Expocentre, Moscow 69

First World War 14, 15
'Floor Ladies' 46
Foreign Trade Ministry 69
French Revolution 14

Georgia 47

'glasnost' 86
Gogol 14
Gorbachev 86
Gorky 14
GUM store 57

Heinz Baked Beans 56
Helsinki 40
Hermitage Museum 94
Hook of Holland 40

Iran 21
Ivan III, 'The Great' 13
Ivan IV, 'The Terrible' 13

KGB 52
Kellogg's Cornflakes 56
Kiev 12
Kievan Rus 12

Lada car 77
Lake Baikal 11
Latvia 18
Lenin 16
Leningrad 82
Lermontov 14
Littlewoods 57
Lithuania 18

Macdonalds 48
Metro 27, 49, 50, 51, 56, 75
Ministry of Foreign Affairs 40, 46
Moldova 20
Mongols 12, 13
Moscow 6, 13, 27, 44, 48, 51, 56, 57, 63, 72, 75, 76, 77, 93, 94

'Near Abroad' 17, 18, 19, 20

Nevsky Prospekt 57, 74, 76, 82
'New Russians' 25
Nicholas II 16
North Caucasus 20

Orthodox Church 13, 36, 73, 84,
        94

Pakistan 21
Pavlovsk 83
'perestroika' 78, 86
Peter the Great 13
Peter the Great's Palace 83
Petrodvorets 83
Pizza Hut 48
Provisional Government 15
Pushkin 14, 93
Pushkin Museum 94

Renaissance 12
Revolution 15
Russian Federation 31
Russian Trade Mission 69

Serfdom 14, 34
Siberia 79
Socialism 36
Soviet Union 10, 17
Soviet Communist 37

State Duma 14
St Basil's Cathedral 42
St Petersburg 8, 13, 27, 44, 48,
        51, 56, 57, 58, 63, 72, t4,
        75, 76, 82, 83, 93, 94
St Petersburg Times 25
Stockholm 25
'Super Rich' 37, 40

Tadzhikistan 20
tapochki 99
Tartars 12
Tilbury 41
Tolstoy 14
Tretyakov Art Gallery 94
troika 94
Tsarism 14, 15
Turgenev 14

Ukraine 18
USSR 10, 17, 21, 47

Visa 39, 40, 44, 68, 69
vodka 28, 49, 66

Women's movement 38

Yeltsin, B.N. 24, 30

Zhirinovsky 29